MW01104329

CIGAR
Asphyxianado

by Eric Spitznagel

Art Direction by Michael Ross

WARNER BOOKS

A Time Warner Company

If you purchase this book without a cover you should be aware that this book may have been stolen property and reported as "unsold and destroyed" to the publisher. In such case neither the author nor the publisher has received any payment for this "stripped book."

Copyright © 1998 by Eric Spitznagel
All rights reserved.

Warner Books, Inc., 1271 Avenue of the Americas, New York, NY 10020
Visit our Web site at
http://warnerbooks.com

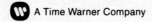 A Time Warner Company

Printed in the United States of America

First Printing: June 1998

10 9 8 7 6 5 4 3 2 1

Library of Congress Cataloging-in-Publication Data
Spitznagel, Eric.
    Cigar asphyxianado / by Eric Spitznagel; art direction by Michael Ross.
        p. cm.
    ISBN 0-446-67409-5
    1. Smoking—Humor. 2. Cigars—Humor. 3. Cigar aficionado—
—Parodies, imitations, etc.   I. Title.
PN6231, S56S65   1998
818'.5407—dc21

Book & Cover design and text composition by Michael Ross
Cover photo by Marty Perez

ATTENTION: SCHOOLS AND CORPORATIONS
WARNER books are available at quantity discounts with bulk purchase for educational, business, or sales promotional use. For information, please write to: SPECIAL SALES DEPARTMENT, WARNER BOOKS, 1271 AVENUE OF THE AMERICAS, NEW YORK, N.Y. 10020

WHO IS THE CIGAR ASPHYXIANADO?

Once considered a dirty habit enjoyed mostly by overweight truckers and corrupt politicians, cigar smoking is now one of the biggest, not to mention *hippest*, pop culture trends of all time. In the last year alone, more than three billion cigars were sold in the United States. Cigar-friendly bars and clubs have sprung up in every major city, and black-tie cigar tastings are suddenly the hottest events in L.A. and New York. Big-time celebrities publicly flaunt their fondness for cigars, and even women have gotten caught up in the craze.

In the middle of it all is *Cigar Asphyxianado*. Thanks to your support, we have become the official mouthpiece of the cigar generation. And I have become a very, very rich man.

What, you may ask, is a Cigar Asphyxianado? What kind of person is he, and how can I be just like him? I'm glad you asked! Contrary to popular belief, the Cigar Asphyxianado is not just somebody who enjoys cigars. Far from it. Asphyxianados understand that smoking cigars makes them more attractive, more intelligent, and generally more sophisticated than the rest of the world. They realize that, as cigar smokers, they are part of an exclusive and very distinguished new American aristocracy.

Marty R. Scanken
Editor-in-Chief of C.A.

Can smoking cigars really change your life? If you don't think so, just look at me! Believe it or not, before becoming a full-time Asphyxianado, I was a lonely man without a friend in the world. I was a middle-aged virgin who lived in his parent's basement, mowed lawns for a living and was often beaten up by violent gangs of prepubescents. Then I discovered cigars and everything changed. I moved out of my parent's house, married a model, became a multimillionaire publisher, and stopped getting beaten up quite as often. Thanks to cigars, I am a connoisseur of the finer things in life. Where once I would have spent my evenings in solitude, eating stale pizza and playing video games, I now loiter at luxurious smoking parties, mingle with celebrities, discuss the leaf-flavors of my favorite brands and flaunt my cigar knowledge to anyone willing to listen.

You too can enjoy this kind of personal metamorphosis. All it takes is a healthy bank account, a flair for pretension, and a subscription to *Cigar Asphyxianado*. Every issue takes you on a fascinating journey into the culture and lifestyle of the modern cigar smoker. There are interviews with the most famous cigar personalities, behind-the-scene reports from the most fashionable cigar events, and invaluable tips that will help you become a popular and worldly Cigar Asphyxianado *just like me!*

Whether you've loved premium cigars all your life or you're just some geek looking for a quick and easy way to get attention, *Cigar Asphyxianado* is the indispensable bible of the exciting and oh-so-chic world of cigars. You might be able to find a more comprehensive guide to cigars, but I can guarantee you this: It will not have as many full-color pictures of celebrities and attractive models sucking on phallic stogies as *Cigar Asphyxianado*. And as any serious smoker will tell you, what else is there?

Marty R. Scanken

Marty R. Scanken
C.A.'s Editor-in-Chief

CIGAR
Asphyxianado

Contents

Outta the Humidor

From Our Readers

Dear Marty,

I picked up a copy of your magazine a few years ago and it inspired me to start smoking cigars. Little did I realize how it would change my life forever. My wife never approved of cigars. She insisted that it was a filthy and worthless habit. I tried to talk to her about it, but she never listened. Every time I lit a cigar, she would scream at me or burst into tears. If I smoked in the house, she would go ballistic and throw dishes and household appliances at me. Sometimes she would force me to smoke outside, even when it was raining or snowing. She was making my life miserable. Then one day she went grocery shopping and never came back. It has been more than a year and I have still not heard from her. Thank you, *Cigar Asphyxianado*. Thank you.

— John Bliss
Chicago, Illinois

Dear Marty,

I've been a smoker for many years and it really annoys me when I'm denied the pleasure of enjoying a fine cigar in public. Most of the time I try to ignore anti-smokers when they complain, but lately they have been pushing me closer and closer to the edge. Last month I was at a five-star restaurant in New York, and after an excellent meal I decided to smoke a cigar. But just seconds after I'd lit up, a woman came over to my table and asked me to extinguish the cigar. She babbled something about it being a non-smoking section and suggested that my cigar was dangerous to her health. Needless to say, I was furious at her intrusion. So I turned to her and thrust my cigar at her face. This struck me as extremely amusing. I thought that burning the smirk off her face was a clever act of social criticism. Apparently I was the only one who held this opinion. The woman started screaming about being "seared" or some such nonsense, and a gentleman from another table ran over and tackled me to the ground. Then the cops showed up and arrested me, claiming that I had "assaulted" the woman. I couldn't believe my ears! This woman had infringed on my rights as a smoker, and yet *I* was the one guilty of assault. It is clear to me that there is still a grossly unfair prejudice against cigar smokers in this country. Unless we stand up for our rights, we will never be allowed to enjoy the freedom of choice that the Constitution guarantees all Americans. I hope that other Asphyxianados like myself will similarly refuse to become victims of the fascist war on cigars.

— Bret Scott
Denver, Colorado

Dear Marty,

I enjoy reading your magazine because it brings back many fond memories from my youth. When I was a kid there was an old woman living next door who everybody called "Crazy Betsy." The adults said she was batty, but she was always very kind to me. I'd see her out in her back yard every morning, puffing on a big cigar and waving to the neighborhood boys. On the weekends my friends and I would go over to her house to help with errands. She had us wash her car or mow her lawn or sometimes even massage her feet. Whatever the chore, she always insisted that we remove our shirts. While we worked, she would sit nearby and watch us intently as she sipped on her whiskey and muttered under her breath. When we were finished, she would invite us into her living room for KoolAid and a playful game of Twister. We always let her win because it seemed to make her happy. As a reward for a hard day's work, she would give each of us one of her cigars. We would smoke them well into the afternoon as our host told us silly pornographic stories about sailors and virgins. To be honest, my friends and I always suspected that she was a little nuts, but we were addicted to those wonderful cigars. I'm not sure what happened to "Crazy Betsy." I've heard rumors that she's in prison today, something to do with a church youth group and some disgruntled parents. But I will always remember those care-free afternoons and the smell of her cigars.

— Sam Mednick
Madison, Wisconsin

Dear Marty,

I was one of the thousands of smokers who participated in *Cigar Asphyxianado*'s March on Washington D.C. last summer. Although we were viciously mocked by the media, I am thrilled that we had the courage to stand up for smokers' rights. It is unfair that cigar smokers are treated like second-class citizens, forced to enjoy our cigars in alleys and bitterly-cold back yards. I can only pray that the bureaucrats in Washington got the message. How could they not have been impressed by our dedication? After all, we marched for almost an entire block — no small feat for serious smokers. "Today we show the world that Asphyxianados will no longer be ignored," you said to the crowd. "We will cough in the face of Lady Liberty until she acknowledges us. We will stand together, united, wheezing as one." It was a truly inspirational speech, and I'm sure the throngs of smokers would have shown their appreciation if they weren't so winded from the march. Thank you for giving this smoker her dignity. You helped fill my black heart with pride.

—Kelly Kreglow
Easton, Pennsylvania

Dear Marty,

Although I am fairly new to the world of cigars, I am as passionate about smoking as even the most educated Asphyxianado. I first discovered cigars by accident, when I was on my honeymoon in the Caribbean. My bride and I had checked into a luxurious honey-moon suite and she suggested that I go out and purchase some wine from a local liquor store. (She is so conservative about money that she refused to pay for the hotel's over-priced selection.) On the way there I passed by a quaint-looking cigar shop and, out of curiosity, walked inside. I was not a cigar smoker at this time, but I was in the mood to celebrate and a cigar seemed like the perfect way to do this. I asked the tobacconist to help me select a cigar and he took me on a fascinating tour of cigar culture and tradition. He taught me how to properly rate the quality of a cigar, how to cut and light them, and how to enjoy them like a true Asphyxianado. We smoked cigars for hours and discussed a wide array of topics, from politics to art history to the American ban on Cuban cigars. I lost track of time and did not make it back to the hotel until well into the morning, where I found my wife delirious with worry and complaining that she had spent the night in tears. I feel guilty that my wife and I never got to enjoy an actual honeymoon, but I have to admit, my enchanting evening of smoking and talking with a knowledgeable tobacconist was well worth the strain on my marriage. I am hoping to take another trip to the Caribbean for our ten-year anniversary. Sadly, my wife has decided not to join me, but I will carry on without her and enjoy what I expect will be a sentimental reunion with the tobacconist who has become my friend and cigar mentor. Perhaps I am just old-fashioned, but I believe that a wedding anniversary is special, and I intend to celebrate mine with a premium cigar.

— John Mulhern
Queens, New York

Dear Marty,

Your advice on buying a private jet ("Your First Private Jet," March, 1997) was one of the most inter-esting and informative articles ever published in *Cigar Asphyxianado.* I was so inspired by the piece that I mortgaged my home and purchased a jet. Am I ever glad I did! I invited a group of friends to join for the inaugural flight and it turned into a memorable experience for all con-cerned. I brought a box of Hoyo de Monterrey Excaliburs for the trip, and despite the fact that none of my friends are smokers, they all sparked up one of these fine cigars. Even the pilot joined in the fes-tivities. We were having such a wonderful time that we didn't realize there was no one flying the plane. Next thing I knew, we crashed into a remote island. Half of my guests were killed and the jet was totally destroyed. Not want-ing to let a little inconvenience ruin an otherwise pleasant afternoon, we lit up more cigars as we fed off the bodies of our dearly departed compadres. I have never before experienced such a warm and un-inhibited gathering. I can only hope that our friendships will continue to blossom long after we are rescued and returned to civilization. Thank you, *Cigar Asphyxianado*, for encouraging us to make memories that will last a lifetime.

— Jason Chin
Somewhere in the South Pacific

CIGAR

*How to Smoke
a Cigar Without
Looking Like
an Idiot*

You've searched high and low for the perfect cigar, and after months of careful study and deliberation, you've finally found it. Now you're sitting in a cigar bar, dressed in your finest smoking garb, ready to light up your precious stogie. But for some reason, you're apprehensive. You've waited for what seems like an eternity for this moment, yet you're frozen in your tracks. You wonder why you can't bring yourself to smoke your hard-earned cigar. This is, after all, what the entire cigar experience is all about. You've gone through the hassle of learning everything there is to know about cigars. This should be the easy part, right?

Wrong!

Your paralyzing fear is justified considering what you are about to endure. Smoking a cigar is not nearly as simple as it sounds. Before you dare to call yourself a true Asphyxianado, you must first become familiar with the "ritual" of smoking. This rite of connoisseurship is one of the cigar culture's most time-honored and intimidating traditions. Not just anybody can perform the ritual correctly. The process is so complex and confusing that even a physics professor would have a difficult time understanding it. But the Asphyxianado realizes the ritual is essential to truly appreciate a premium cigar. Failing to adhere to this strict criterion results in an inferior smoking experience or, even worse, severe mockery from your peers and possible exile from the cigar community.

Before you attempt to smoke your first cigar, heed the following advice, study it well, and may God save your soul.

PART ONE: CUTTING THE CIGAR

The first and most important step in smoking a cigar is the delicate surgery known as "cutting the head." Your first instinct may be to bite off the cap with your teeth like Clint Eastwood did in all those spaghetti Westerns. This is not recommended behavior and would never be practiced by any dignified Asphyxianado. While it is true that this method has a certain dangerous quality that cigar smokers find attractive, it bears mentioning that the rugged characters portrayed by Mr. Eastwood would never be invited to sit in the VIP lounge of an expensive cigar-friendly restaurant.

In almost every case, a Cigar Asphyxianado will use an ordinary pocketknife to cut his cigar. They're plain yet elegant, common yet classy, and very, *very* difficult to use. Most knives are not designed to cut the multi-textured leaves of a cigar wrapper, and attempting to use them for that purpose can be a frustrating and hopeless endeavor. This is exactly the reason Asphyxianados like them so much. They are attracted to this impossible challenge. They relish the fact that most people are not brave or stupid enough to use them. And they giddily anticipate the opportunity to once again prove their superiority.

Rest assured, it *can* be done — if you're willing to take the time to learn the proper procedure. So grab yourself a knife, take a few deep breaths, think nice, happy thoughts, and let's get started.

9

CUTTING A CIGAR USING ONLY A RUSTY OLD POCKETKNIFE

Holding the cigar firmly in one hand, pull the knife towards you as if peeling an apple. Completely rotate the cigar while gently cutting into the cap.

You will probably pull the knife too hard, causing it to slip and slice into your thumb. This is to be expected. Be sure to keep the injured appendage well away from the cigar, so as not to bleed all over the wrapper.

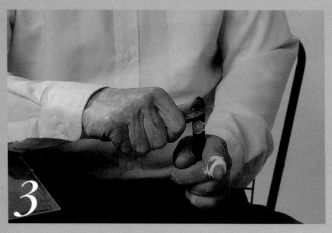

After bandaging the wound, attempt to make a cut once again, this time pressing the cigar against a flat surface to get more leverage.

This time you will cut too far into the cigar and break the connection between the wrapper and binder. The cigar will begin to unravel and the tobacco leaves will spill out.

In a fit of rage, stab the cigar repeatedly, cutting it into shreds.

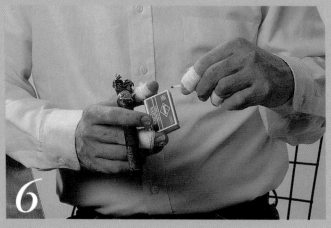

Light and enjoy!

PART TWO: LIGHTING THE CIGAR

There has been much debate about what instruments should be used to light a cigar. The only agreed-upon rule is that you should never *ever* use a fluid lighter. Fluid lighters can poison the taste of a cigar, giving it the nasty flavor of gasoline. If you simply must use a fluid lighter, only use a Zippo. This is not to suggest that Zippos are any better than other lighters, but they are more expensive and they tend to make loud, metallic clicks when opened. Although not the best method, Zippo lighters are arguably the hippest, and some say well worth a few noxious fumes in your cigar.

Paper matches are virtually useless because they don't burn long enough to light a cigar, not to mention being completely devoid of elegance. Purists light their cigars with a sliver of cedar from the cigar box, called a "spill." Not only is this the best way to light a cigar, it also demonstrates that you are classier than most smokers. Because you can only get these cedar matches from a cigar box, everyone will know that you buy your stogies in large quantities, which only very rich or obsessive smokers can afford. Also, prying a match from the cedar wall is a difficult and monotonous process,

which only a serious Asphyx-ianado would be willing to do. A handmade cedar match tells the world that you care about smoking so much that you are willing to waste an entire weekend painstakingly crafting the perfect match. Coincidentally, it is also a way of saying "I have no friends, no job and I am very, very lonely." But that is another story.

Once you have decided what type of lighting instrument to use, it is time to begin the slow and arduous process of actually lighting the cigar. You can always recognize beginner smokers by how long it takes them to light their cigars. If you find that you can get a cigar going in a few minutes, then you can be certain that you are doing it wrong

and any cultivated smoker is probably laughing at you.

To light a cigar like an Asphyx-ianado takes time, a really, *really* long time. Make sure that you have no commitments in the foreseeable future, because you are probably not going to make it. If you don't have the time or

patience to light a cigar the way it should be done, then perhaps you don't have what it takes to become an Asphyx-ianado and should probably take up a less refined hobby, like chess or laying asphalt.

The choice is up to you.

The Proper Procedure for Lighting a Cigar

1. Hold the flame just below the tobacco, not allowing it to come into contact with the cigar. Angle the cigar 30° below horizontal, but no more. If you point the cigar down too steeply, the flame will run up the sides of the barrel and char the wrapper. Keep the flame small, no more than 3/8" to 1/2" high. Hold the flame tip at exactly 1/4" below the lower rim of the foot. Straying from these measurements by even a fraction of an inch can totally ruin a cigar and you must dispose of it immediately.

2. As the flame gently licks the foot, rotate the cigar counterclockwise with your fingers while taking very short

puffs on the cigar. Make two rotations every 28 seconds and then look at the end of the cigar to check on your progress. Continue this process for ten minutes, not a second more. Remember, you are *not* lighting the cigar yet. You are only "introducing" it to the flame. If the wrapper catches fire, you have failed miserably.

3. Having completed the preliminary lighting, place the cigar on the end of a table and leave it there for twenty minutes to an hour. This gives the cigar time to adjust to the heat and allows you an opportunity to get a few stiff drinks to steady your nerves.

4. Return to the cigar and resume lighting it, this time holding the flame slightly closer to the head but no more than 1/3" below the foot. Rotate the cigar slowly under the flame, taking as long as thirty minutes to make a complete rotation. After a few hours of this, you should notice that the rim is beginning to turn gray. You'll see a tiny wisp of smoke curling up from the cigar, no higher than 5 to 6 inches and 1/2" in diameter, drifting ever so slightly to your left. If the smoke does not follow these specifications, you either have a faulty cigar or you have done something horribly, horribly wrong. Dispose of the cigar at once.

5. Having successfully heated the cigar, the next step is to ignite the binder — the cigar's fuse — which will carry the flame down the cigar's length. Begin by positioning the flame under the cigar's left side (the side closest to the equator), gently toasting it for at least two hours. It is extremely important that you keep your hand steady. Just a slight muscle twitch could result in the flame burning too deeply into the cigar, causing an uncontrollable tobacco fire that will not only ruin the cigar, but might put your fellow smokers in danger. If this happens, dispose of the cigar at once!

6. After the left side of the cigar has been lit, set it aside and allow the flame to "sink in" for about three hours.

7. Repeat step #5 for the right side. Take another three-hour break.

8. Now things get slightly complicated. Angle the cigar 25° below horizontal and hold the flame exactly 1/3" below the foot. Rotate the cigar under the flame, alternating between clockwise and counterclockwise, allowing 23 seconds for the clockwise rotations and 29 seconds for counterclockwise, while puffing the cigar every two to four minutes (depending on the room temperature). Continue this process for 43 minutes.

9. If the foot has not become cherry red, you may need to blow on it to accelerate things. Send a gentle breeze of air toward the cigar at approximately 21 MPH. If the cigar is crackling and spitting sparks of fire, it is probably lacking moisture. It is not too late to remedy this. Place your tongue directly on the flame, holding it there for at least ten minutes but possibly as long as an hour, depending on the degree of moisture needed.

10. Although the cigar may appear to be completely lit, your job is not yet done. Like an antique car, a cigar needs a strong kick-start to get it moving. This can be accomplished by firmly grasping the head of the cigar with your mouth and sucking in the smoke. Continue sucking for exactly 12 minutes (or 13 minutes if you live on the east coast) without a break. Some of the smoke may get into your lungs, so don't be alarmed if you begin to feel dizzy and nauseous. It's a small price to pay for successfully lighting a premium cigar.

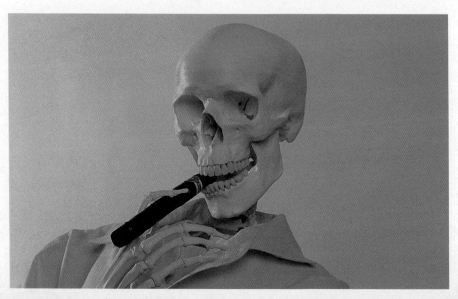

$\mathscr{T}$he best way to say, "I'm rich and you're not!"

Let's face it, you're rich. You've got the kind of disposable income that allows you to enjoy the finer things in life. You have homes on both coasts and a yacht in every port. You buy and sell people like cattle and you're never without a beautiful woman on your arm. You're arrogant and egotistical and there are few people who'd claim to be your friend. But quite frankly... you're too rich to care.

RICH BASTARD cigars are made just for you. They aren't the best cigars available but they are the most expensive. A single box of these hand-crafted stogies costs more than feeding a family of four for a year. You couldn't make a more frivolous purchase if you tried. But you can afford to spend recklessly, and best of all, you can afford to be smug about it. After all... it *is* your money.

RICH
BASTARD
CIGARS

For people who are wealthy enough to waste their money.

A Comic and His Exploding Cigars

The Comedy Genius of Buzzy Klein

Buzzy Klein (right) and then-partner Slappy McDonald. Judging by the lack of scarring on Buzzy's face, vaudeville historians estimate this picture was taken in 1923.

No one remembers Franko "Buzzy" Klein anymore. The comedian who was once hailed as the unfunniest actor ever to perform in vaudeville, TV and film has become a virtual nonentity. Not only has he been forgotten by audiences, but by comedy historians as well. Why has the legacy of this not-so-great actor been swept under the carpet? Why have we denied Buzzy Klein his rightful place in the annals of mediocre American comedy? Nobody knows, and apparently, nobody cares.

Buzzy Klein first got into show business in the early 1920s, playing the straight man to the now legendary Slappy McDonald. Audiences roared as Buzzy endured countless humiliations at the hands of Slappy, from pies in the face to hammers in the groin to

having his internal organs surgically removed and then set on fire. For a while, Buzzy and Slappy were one of the most popular comedy teams in vaudeville.

But with stardom just around the corner, Slappy was seduced by Hollywood and left the act to pursue a career in films. Buzzy attempted to do the same, but no studio would hire him. So Buzzy returned to vaudeville and began performing as a solo act. Without Slappy by his side, the magic was gone. Audiences were more disturbed than amused by Buzzy's one-man show, which consisted primarily of Buzzy punching himself in the face and screaming "Bad Buzzy, bad Buzzy!" Buzzy's career in show business appeared to be dead.

But in 1932, Buzzy made a

dramatic comeback, appearing in his first feature film: *The Man With the Exploding Cigar*. Merv Salisberg, the producer who re-discovered Buzzy, said he knew Buzzy was destined to be a star when he first laid eyes on him.

"He was performing on the streets for change," remembers Salisberg. "It was basic vaudeville shtick. He'd slap his face or fall to the ground and flail his arms like an idiot. Nothing too impressive. But there was one part of his act that really got me. He lit a cigar and the damn thing blew up in his face. It was the funniest thing I'd ever seen in my life. His whole head was on fire and he was running around screaming for somebody to help him. Buzzy told me later that he didn't know the cigar was going to blow up like that.

Three Classic Scenes

Three of Buzzy and Slappy's vaudeville sketches are still used as textbook examples by comedy writers. Shown below are: 1) The Walking Sketch, 2) The Newspaper Sketch, and 3) The Telephone Sketch.

1) The Walking Sketch

2) The Newspaper Sketch

3) The Telephone Sketch

Apparently somebody slipped him an exploding cigar as a joke. I guess that makes sense because Buzzy, left to his own devices, wasn't very clever."

The Man With the Exploding Cigar was a huge box office smash, and Buzzy was hailed by critics as "hilariously pathetic." Even today, the film still holds up as a classic farce. Buzzy plays a lovable tramp who searches the world for a good cigar, but every one he finds blows up in his face. Audiences howled with laughter at Buzzy's misadventures, and every studio in Hollywood wanted to put him in their films.

Buzzy stayed with the director and studio that gave him a chance, and the following year he appeared in *Another Man With Another Exploding Cigar*. The film did moderately well, but it was clear that film audiences were growing tired of the exploding cigar bit. His third film, which premiered in 1938, was *The Man With the Exploding Necktie*. It closed in only a week.

"It was a dreadful film," says Betty Doherty, the actress who co-starred with Buzzy in *Exploding Necktie*. "I knew it was going to bomb before we even finished making it. The problem was, Buzzy just didn't know anything about comedy. All he knew how to do was injure himself, and that can get really old after a while. If he forgot his lines or felt that he was performing badly, he'd pick up any object he could find and start beating himself

Toward the end of their partnership, Slappy would improvise freely, often knocking Buzzy out cold before the gruesome act could be completed. Says Slappy, "The audience got jumpy, but I never worried about hurting Buzzy. Buzzy was a clotter."

Buzzy's attempt at a solo act included the sketch "Man of Many Vices." Though a favorite of Buzzy's, it roused only indifference in the audience.

on the head with it. He thought that would make people like him. He had no idea what he was doing."

Once again, Buzzy's career was finished and he disappeared from the public eye. Until 1956, the year of Buzzy's third comeback. Perhaps out of nostalgia for the years of vaudeville, Buzzy was given his own game show, *You Bet My Life*. Contestants were interviewed by Buzzy and, if they said the "magic word," were allowed to smack Buzzy repeatedly with a huge rubber chicken. The show was moderately successful for a few years, if only because audiences were intrigued by the sight of a grown man being beaten by a chicken. But after two seasons the novelty was gone, and

Buzzy's first (and last) TV show was canceled.

Buzzy made one final attempt to become a star in 1992, at the ripe old age of 96. He planned to return to the stage in a one-man show off-off-Broadway called *The Exploding Cigar and I*. But while rehearsing the comedy routine that had made him temporarily famous, he died when one of his exploding cigars blew him, and the theater, into a million pieces. According to police reports, Buzzy had accidentally loaded his cigar with too much TNT, a tragic mistake that insured he would never again attempt a comeback.

"Buzzy would have wanted it that way," says Audrey Klein, his wife of sixty years. "His explod-

ing cigar was the only thing that got him any kind of attention. It's kind of fitting that the gag that made him a star also took his life. He would have appreciated the irony of that. Actually, he probably wouldn't. He wasn't very good with irony. He wasn't very good with comedy in general. But if somebody had appreciated the irony for him, that would've made him happy."

Buzzy Klein may not be considered a great comedian. In fact, he may not even be considered at all. But for Asphyxianados who have often wondered, "Wouldn't it be funny if this cigar blew up in my face?" Buzzy offered an answer that was both profound and hilarious.

Kinda.

Tonight is special.
Share it with someone you love.

Romantico Cigars
are more than
just a satisfy-
ing smoke.
They're also
a compan-
ion. They'll
listen to you.
They'll care
about your
needs. They won't
say "I love you" unless
they really mean it. They
won't leave town when the
relationship becomes too intense.
And best of all, they'll never cheat on you with
another woman. They're your lover *and* your best friend.

Romantico Cigars

QUALITY CIGARS FOR LONELY WOMEN

BLIND TASTING

With the glut of new cigar brands introduced each year, it's impossible for even the most knowledgeable Asphyxianado to make an educated cigar selection. Left to your own devices, it would take nearly twenty years and millions of dollars to sample every cigar currently on the marketplace. But the writers at *Cigar Asphyxianado* have a lot of money and a lot of free time. We've done your cigar homework for you, spending countless hours smoking hundreds of cigars so that you, our loyal readers, are more informed.

For this issue, we sampled some of the very best new cigars on the market. As with all of our blind taste tests, we use a standard rating system that answers the questions every cigar smoker needs to know. Is the cigar expensive or really expensive? What color mucus does the cigar produce? How long does the cigar's stench stay on your clothes? And on a scale of 1 to 10 (10 being highest), just how envious will your peers be of your cigar selection? We also include comments and unintelligible gibberish from our panel of experts. Their insights are guaranteed to make no sense whatsoever, so you just know it's deep.

S. UPMARR

Panetela   Cuba

PRICE RANGE: very expensive   PHLEGM COLOR: yellow
ODOR LIFE-SPAN: four months   ENVY FACTOR: 7

"There is a pervasive Marxist quality to it, although the filler has hints of a Christian morality."

RATING: 88

ROMEO Y ROMEO

Homosexion No. 3   Nicaragua

PRICE RANGE: expensive   PHLEGM COLOR: greenish-yellow
ODOR LIFE-SPAN: six weeks   ENVY FACTOR: 4

"An agreeable smoke with rich, nutty flavors that are satisfying without being historically irrelevant."

RATING: 81

MELAN DE NOMA

Havana Reserve Toro   Honduras

PRICE RANGE: off the scale   PHLEGM COLOR: greenish-purple
ODOR LIFE-SPAN: fourteen months   ENVY FACTOR: 8

"A draw that is wry and puckish, with pleasing overtones of irony in the aftertaste."

RATING: 85

ASSTON

Double Magnum   Dom. Rep.

PRICE RANGE: very expensive   PHLEGM COLOR: hot pink
ODOR LIFE-SPAN: eleven months   ENVY FACTOR: 8

"A complicated cigar with strong, spicy notes that just don't make sense, even in the Catholic context."

RATING: 89

EL REY STINKO

Especial no. 281   Cuba

PRICE RANGE: off the scale   PHLEGM COLOR: orangish-green
ODOR LIFE-SPAN: twenty-four months   ENVY FACTOR: 9

"A smooth, medium-bodied smoke with a pungent aroma that offers an unbearable reminder of mortality."

RATING: 91

RABID DOG

Robusto No. 7   Jamaica

PRICE RANGE: very expensive   PHLEGM COLOR: turquoise
ODOR LIFE-SPAN: six to eight months   ENVY FACTOR: 8

"Clearly an act of social criticism, this mellow smoke has a creamy aftertaste that makes a convincing argument for political unification."

RATING: 86

HOYO DE MOTOR CITY

No. 5   Detroit

PRICE RANGE: expensive   PHLEGM COLOR: shit brown
ODOR LIFE-SPAN: 108 months   ENVY FACTOR: 3

"A somber, almost melancholy cigar that leaves just a touch of ennui on the palate."

RATING: 79

Don't Believe the Hype

A Doctor Examines the Dubious Link Between Cigars and Bad Health

by Jamie Veiss, M.D.

I have been a cigar smoker for fifty years. But in this day and age, when most of the world believes that tobacco is a serious health menace, it is difficult to enjoy an occasional cigar without criticism, especially if you work in a medical field. As a doctor, I am constantly confronted by my colleagues, who suggest that I am sending the wrong message to my patients by smoking cigars. I tell them what I tell everyone, "Prove to me that cigars are bad for your health and I will quit." Of course, they can't.

Occasionally, I will meet a doctor who insists there is hard evidence that cigars are deadly. They cite the hundreds of studies that link tobacco with a staggering array of health problems like cancer, chronic bronchitis, emphysema and many more too numerous to mention. While these medical conjectures are generally accepted as facts, I like to remind my detractors that in Nazi Germany during the 30s and 40s, it was also accepted as "fact" that Jews were evil and even dangerous. I think my

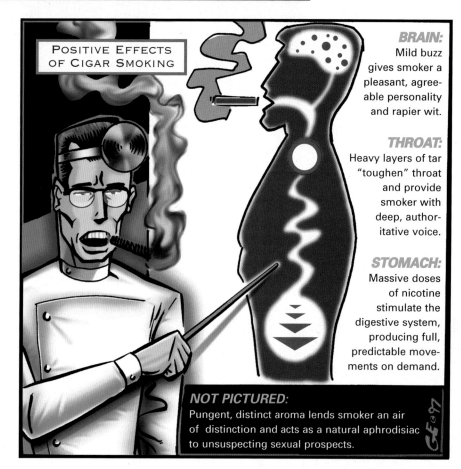

POSITIVE EFFECTS OF CIGAR SMOKING

BRAIN: Mild buzz gives smoker a pleasant, agreeable personality and rapier wit.

THROAT: Heavy layers of tar "toughen" throat and provide smoker with deep, authoritative voice.

STOMACH: Massive doses of nicotine stimulate the digestive system, producing full, predictable movements on demand.

NOT PICTURED: Pungent, distinct aroma lends smoker an air of distinction and acts as a natural aphrodisiac to unsuspecting sexual prospects.

point is obvious.

But why, you may ask, would our doctors tell us that cigars are bad for us if they aren't? What do they have to gain by convincing a nation of smokers to scorn their cigars and find more healthy habits? It saddens me to say this, but I suspect that many of my peers in the medical community have been corrupted by power

and money. They have been influenced by politicians with anti-tobacco agendas to spread misinformation about cigars to you, the American public. The "facts" you have been fed about cigars are not based on real evidence at all, but have been fabricated by Washington bureaucrats who, for one reason or another, want us to stop smoking.

Am I suggesting that doctors — maybe even your doctor — is accepting illegal bribes from the government to denounce cigars? I wish it was that simple, but I'm afraid that the answer is even more sinister than any of us would like to believe. From what I have been able to gather from my years of research, the White House is practicing some sort of brain control on our scientists and doctors, turning them into zombies who will say and do exactly what they are told.

Nonsense, you say? The delusional ramblings of a clearly paranoid man? Perhaps. But consider this: In 1963, President John F. Kennedy was assassinated — only two years after he proclaimed a trade embargo with Cuba. According to some Kennedy historians, the president was considering lifting the embargo just months before his ill-fated trip to Dallas. Despite the political tensions between the U.S. and Cuba, he did not feel right denying his countrymen access to Cuban cigars. Is it a coincidence that Kennedy was killed before he had a chance to legalize Cuban cigars and that every president elected since Kennedy has been an ardent non-smoker? Isn't it possible that our government might be controlled by a group of health-nut zealots (perhaps the Masons) who have conspired for over forty years to rid the world of the tobacco product that threatens their autarchic power?

Or consider this. In 1947, an air force pilot named Kenneth Arnold was flying over the Cascade Mountains when he spotted an unidentified flying object which he described as "cigar-shaped." Since then, hundreds of witnesses have also seen these cigar-like objects, and some believe that they might be extraterrestrial spaceships. We have still received no explanation from the government, which continues to deny the existence of U.F.O.s or claim that the sightings were caused by weather balloons or grain alcohol. They refuse to even consider the most obvious explanation: these airborne cigars are proof of intelligent life from another planet, an intelligent life that not only smokes cigars but has learned how to fly them. Who else but a government with an odious prejudice against cigars would try to hide this information from the public?

I realize that by writing this article I have put my own life in danger. I suspect that my phone has already been tapped and I have reason to believe that my mailman may actually be a robot spy for the CIA. I may have to leave the country until the truth behind this governmental deception is revealed. But I pray that you, my brothers and sisters at *Cigar Asphyxianado*, will carry on the good fight until I return. Trust no one. Watch your backs. The truth is out there. And may god have mercy on our souls.

Dr. Veiss is professor of pathology and conspiracy theories at the Montana Institute of Health Sciences Center.

you've lost your job
your wife has left you
your kids hate your guts

time for a cigar.   ASSTON
                     Cigars

Life is shit. Treat yourself to something special.

A Cigar Star Is Born

Jack Willison Smokes His Way Back Into the Hollywood Limelight

To relax, Willison takes time out of his busy schedule to share a stogie with his Boston terrier, Dillinger.

Jack Willison is sitting in a diner with his friends, smoking cigars. A waitress comes over and tells them that cigars are not allowed in their establishment. Willison refuses to put out his cigar, so the waitress asks him to leave. Outraged, Willison jumps on top of the table and begins smashing plates with his boots.

"You can take my cigar and stick it up your ass," he screams.

You may recognize this as the infamous scene from *Biker Scum*, the 1971 film that introduced Jack Willison to the world. It was the beginning of a stellar career that would see him take over Hollywood and become the quintessential leading man.

Although he has demonstrated an uncanny versatility in his numerous acting roles, Willison is best known for playing "tough guy" characters. Some of his most memorable roles include the gun-toting loner of *Bus Driver* (1975), the manic depressive detective of *Chinese Gangsters Are Big Trouble* (1983) and the smartly-dressed pimp of *Hooker-Rama* (1991). His characters understand the hard-knock life of the street and enjoy engaging in senseless violence for the sheer thrill of it. They drive cars through buildings, seduce mafia mistresses, shoot wildly into crowds and, of course, smoke cigars.

Cigars are the most defining characteristic of Willison's characters. In almost every one of his films he has a stogie in his mouth and a smile on his face. There is something about cigars that make Willison more appealing to audiences. Perhaps it's the element of danger that cigars give his characters. Or perhaps it's the flirty wheeze that has become Willison's trademark. Whatever the reason, Willison and cigars are a match made in heaven.

This year Willison is starring in *Bloody Justice*, the story of a cocky undercover cop who single-handedly takes on the Chicago mob. Hollywood insiders are already predicting that the film will be another hit for "Action Jack." We talked to Willison in his Beverly Hills home about his career, his new film, and his love for premium cigars.

CIGAR ASPHYXIANADO: How long have you been a cigar smoker?

WILLISON: Well, to tell you the truth, I don't really care for cigars. I don't mind them or anything. If someone's smoking a cigar, I won't protest. But I don't like to smoke them myself.

CIGAR ASPHYXIANADO: Your passion for cigars is legendary. Rumor has it that you're hardly ever without a stogie in your mouth, even on the set of your movies.

WILLISON: I wouldn't say

Willison's first bit part in a film came at age nineteen as the naughty bellboy in Ho Chi Mihn Hotel. *(1969)*
CIGAR COUNT: 2

Unfulfilled by film stardom, Jack tackled Broadway in David Mamin's Angry Chicago Salesmen. *(1977)*
CIGAR COUNT: 0

Willison's biggest box office success came as a cold-blooded killer with a heart of gold in Tender Valley. *(1982)*
CIGAR COUNT: 4

Jack's critics will never let him live down his ill-fated foray into television, Fishing with Willison. *(1986)*
CIGAR COUNT: 3-4 per episode

that I have a passion for cigars. I smoke in my movies, but that's just when the script calls for it. It's my *characters* who smoke cigars, not me.

CIGAR ASPHYXIANADO: What is your favorite brand of cigar?

WILLISON: I don't have a favorite brand. I just smoke whatever the prop guys give me. I don't really know that much about cigars.

CIGAR ASPHYXIANADO: Do your prefer Churchills or Robustos?

WILLISON: I'm sorry, I really don't know the difference. Like I said, I just smoke whatever they give me. I don't usually look at the brand names.

CIGAR ASPHYXIANADO: I tend to prefer Churchills. They're a more smooth-tasting smoke without such a sharp bite on the finish. Don't you agree?

WILLISON: Uh, I guess. I really have no idea.

CIGAR ASPHYXIANADO: Tell us about your new movie, Bloody Justice.

WILLISON: Well, it's about this undercover cop whose partner was killed by a mob hitman, and he decides...

CIGAR ASPHYXIANADO: Does he smoke cigars?

A self-described "health freak," Willison works out up to four hours per day, going through an average of nine Hoya del Gringos in a given workout session.

WILLISON: What? Oh, yes, he does, but that doesn't —

CIGAR ASPHYXIANADO: Fascinating. What kind of cigars does he smoke?

WILLISON: I don't know.

CIGAR ASPHYXIANADO: Did you decide to do this movie because the character smokes cigars?

WILLISON: No, not at all. I loved the script and I wanted to try an action film again. Cigars had nothing to do with it.

CIGAR ASPHYXIANADO: It seems that a lot of movies these days have characters who smoke cigars. Do you think Hollywood is trying to cash in on the popularity of cigars, or do they just love cigars as much as we do?

WILLISON: I don't think it has anything to do with that. Some scripts just *happen* to have characters who just *happen* to smoke cigars. No writer puts cigars in a script because they think it'll be hip. That's just stupid.

CIGAR ASPHYXIANADO: Do a lot of your actor friends smoke cigars?

WILLISON: Some of them do, some of them don't. I don't really notice. It's not that big a deal.

CIGAR ASPHYXIANADO: Do you have any contacts in Cuba?

WILLISON: How do you mean?

CIGAR ASPHYXIANADO: Where do you get your Cuban cigars?

WILLISON: I don't smoke Cuban cigars. I don't smoke *any* cigars. Even if I did, what makes you think I'd be able to get Cuban cigars?

CIGAR ASPHYXIANADO: Your last movie, Monkey Madness, *was shot in Cuba. Didn't you pick up some cigars while you were there, or maybe meet some locals who could set you up with a steady supply of Cuban cigars?*

WILLISON: No. I don't smoke cigars. I told you that already. Would you please stop asking me about cigars? I'd much rather talk about my new movie.

CIGAR ASPHYXIANADO: I see. Some people say that your career is washed up.

WILLISON: Yes, I know. But I think *Bloody Justice* will prove them wrong.

CIGAR ASPHYXIANADO: You're hoping that this film will give you a second chance at stardom?

WILLISON: I'm expecting it to. It's a very good movie.

Wearing his pimp hat from Hooker-Rama, *Jack prepares his vegetarian breakfast: egg whites with fresh zucchini and tofu sausage. Says Jack, "My body keeps me in business, and I can't contaminate it with any crap." (Shown here with a De La Gorda.)*

"I...smoke...much...cigars." — JACK WILLISON

CIGAR ASPHYXIANADO: Bloody Justice *could very likely become a huge success, if it gets enough publicity.*

WILLISON: I suppose that's how it works.

CIGAR ASPHYXIANADO: You know, we're thinking of making this interview a cover story.

WILLISON: That would be nice.

CIGAR ASPHYXIANADO: A lot of people read our magazine. A lot of potential ticket buyers.

WILLISON: Yes, I know.

CIGAR ASPHYXIANADO: But you know, this is *a magazine about cigars.*

WILLISON: I understand that. But I don't want to—

CIGAR ASPHYXIANADO: The way we see it, if you scratch our back, we'll scratch yours.

WILLISON: (*After a long pause*) I see what you're getting at.

CIGAR ASPHYXIANADO: Shall we begin again?

WILLISON: Sure.

CIGAR ASPHYXIANADO: How many cigars do you smoke in an average day?

WILLISON: At least twenty or thirty.

CIGAR ASPHYXIANADO: Mr. Willison, you are truly a Cigar Asphyxianado!

Look into his eyes and tell him you don't want his cigar.

Hoyo de Motor City cigars are not made with expensive, high-tech equipment like most of the more popular brands. Our cigars are hand-rolled by impoverished street urchins in a disgusting Detroit sweatshop. They get paid ten cents an hour, which they use to feed and clean their miserable little bodies. Their life is hard, but it could be a lot worse. Without Hoyo de Motor City, these victims of society would probably starve to death out in the mean streets, another casualty of a cruel and uncaring world.

HOYO DE MOTOR CITY CIGARS
SMOKE THEM FOR THE CHILDREN

My Weekend in the Holy Land

by Marty Scanken

C.A.'s Editor-in-Chief makes a pilgrimage to the sacred soil of Cuba.

It is a scorching hot morning in Havana. The sweat pours off my body like rafts full of refugees fleeing their homeland. I am jet-lagged from the long journey, and my bowels are loudly rejecting the unpalatable provisions I consumed just hours ago. But despite my physical discomfort, I am happy — happier than I have ever been in my entire life. I have arrived in the country that has beckoned me with its siren song since I was a young boy. I am in Cuba, the land of communism, green fatigues and — most famously — excellent cigars.

I have paid handsomely for this trip, but it is worth every penny. Although I've only been here for less than a day, I am already in love with this land and its grubby people. A Cuban schoolboy has agreed to act as my guide for twenty schillings, and he promises to take me to the finest cigar factory in all of Havana. I can hardly believe my good luck. Finally, I am going to witness firsthand how Cuban cigars are really made! My extremities are tingling with anticipation. It takes us almost three days to reach our destination, but I don't mind the journey. I am willing to travel to the ends of the earth for a chance to enjoy a few puffs from a genuine Cuban cigar.

Reaching the white-stoned terrace of the sweatshop, I can hear salsa music blasting out of the large, smoke-stained windows.

Peeking through one of them, I spot dozens of crusty old women hard at work. They sit in rows on closely spaced wooden benches and tirelessly roll cigar after cigar. Behind them is a large, shirtless man in a black hood, who menaces the workers with a leather whip when they slow down or show signs of fatigue.

A tear comes to my eye as I watch these women. Their world is as perfect as I had imagined. The beautiful squalor they live in and their dedication to the fine art of making cigars is the stuff of story-book legend. Sure, they're miserable, but their misery is the kind that can easily be romanticized from afar.

I enter the workroom from the main entrance and the women welcome me with enthusiasm. Their cries of "Help me" and "Take me with you to America" assure me that they are not opposed to unannounced guests. After the guard beats them into submission, they return to their work as I watch with awe. The air is thick with a bewitching odor of sewage and tobacco. I cannot imagine anything that could heighten the euphoria of this moment — except, perhaps, if I could smoke a freshly rolled cigar. I grab a cigar from the table and light it, sucking in the intoxicating smoke. I am drunk with pleasure and weep openly, unashamed to let my appreciation be known to these lowly peasants.

Each day hundreds of craftspeople — women and children — work in the cigar sweatshops of Havana, producing more than 60 million cigars. Although Cuban cigars have been banned in America since the Kennedy trade embargo of the 60s, the demand for these cigars in the rest of the world is overwhelming.

"Everybody wants a cigar from Havana," says Francisco Padrona, the president of a marketing and distribution company for Cuban cigars. "And to be honest, they're not that good. But you know what? People will buy them anyway. We could, and sometimes do, fill our cigars with leaves, wood chips or old razor blades, and people would still smoke them. We could soak them in bleach or store them in musty basements for years and people would still line up for miles just to touch them. The Queen of England once paid five thousand pounds for a Cuban cigar that I had shoved up my ass. We can do whatever we want with our cigars, because we're Cubans."

Although this year's tobacco harvest is said to be the most bountiful yet, many Cuban cigar factories will be suffering because of a shortage of experienced rollers. According to José Fabio, the director of the factory I visited, there are only so many workers left who have the skills to make a cigar in the traditional manner. "There

In my eagerness to feel an actual Cuban tobacco leaf, I mistakenly stroked a dangerous indigenous plant known as "Muerte Verde," or Green Death. The hives, bloating, and oozing pustules that ensued were a small price to pay during my journey of discovery.

aren't many young people in Cuba these days who are interested in becoming a professional cigar roller," says Fabio. "They complain that the pay is too low and the hours are too long. And they don't care much for all the beatings that go along with the job. At the rate our workers are dying off we may be out of business in a few years."

There probably isn't any danger of that, as long as the demand for Cuban cigars remains consistent. Francisco Padrona claims that some factories are experimenting with alternative means of cigar rolling. One such factory has had limited success with monkeys. "The cigars don't always turn out right," says Padrona. "Sometimes they're rolled unevenly. Sometimes they don't have enough tobacco in them. We even discovered that some monkey-rolled cigars had

been filled with animal feces. We're still getting the kinks out. But like I said before, regardless of the quality, they'll sell."

After José Fabio shows me around his factory, he invites me to sample an S. Upmarr, the most popular cigar made in Cuba. I snatch it out of his hand before he can reconsider his offer. It is indeed a spectacular cigar, with a full-bodied taste and rich aroma that smells suspiciously like burning garbage. But I am so happy to be smoking a cigar that is unavailable to my Asphyxianado brothers back home that I don't dare question my benefactor. Fabio smiles as he observes the eagerness with which I smoke his cigar.

"I'm glad you like it," he says.

"You know, it's Castro's favorite cigar as well. He has a box of them delivered from this factory every week."

My face goes pale. Just hearing his name makes me tremble like a little girl on prom night. Fidel Castro. The leader of Cuba and lover of cigars. The man who started it all. The Asphyxianado who defines all Asphyxianados. I have never met the man, but I often dream of him. In my dreams, he floats over me like an angel and showers me with premium cigars. He picks me up in his strong arms and carries me back to his palace, where cigars and sweaty men live together in peace. It drives me crazy with desire to know that I am smoking one of Fidel's cigars. I feel that much closer to the legendary figure who has turned this boy into a man.

"Could I meet him?" I ask, my voice trembling. Fabio nods, and I begin to weep again. I fall to the ground and kiss Fabio's feet. The rapture is too much for me, and I pass out from exhaustion. It is hours later before I wake up and realize that it was not a dream. I am going to meet Fidel Castro, El Presidente!

I am instructed to wait at my hotel and Fidel's "people" will contact me. Rain and stillness fill the air as I pace the room and consider the miraculous event that is about to happen to me. Little Marty Scanken, the man who was once voted "Most Likely to Work at a Fast Food Chain" by his high school classmates, is going to have a private audience with Fidel Castro. I whisper his name,

hoping to make this dramatic turn of events seem more real. "Fidel. Fidel. Oh my sweet Fidel." My hot breath fogs the windows of my room, and I write his name on the mist with my finger. "Fidel," I write. "You are the temptress of my— "

There is a loud knock at the door. It is the Foreign Affairs official, who tells me it is time to meet... Fidel.

"Are you ready?" she asks.

"As ready as I'll ever be," I reply. "Hold me."

Resisting my hug, she directs me down the front steps of the hotel into the busy afternoon streets. Waiting by the curb is a limo. I am pushed into the car by a group of thugs and we

On advice from his Minister of Exports, El Presidente will only be photographed while wearing a bandolier of his favorite stogies, S. Upmarr Cigars. The Minister feels that this will both "raise awareness of Cuban Cigar quality" to smokers worldwide, and "frustrate the piss out of" embargo-deprived Asphyxianados here in the States.

Fidel proudly boasts that Cuban cigars are healthier than cigars from other nations, due to the fact that he has "outlawed all cancers of the lips, mouth, throat, and lungs." Contraction of these types of cancer is now punishable by death.

33

Overwhelmed to finally meet the legendary Fidel Castro, I forgot myself, and began to voraciously lick his stogie in subservience. The subsequent kick in the ribs I received was sobering, yet playful.

his suggestion at my next editorial meeting, but he just laughs. He asks about my readers, wanting to know if they have "big asses like you." This makes the soldiers roar with laughter, so I join in. I do not understand this Cuban humor, but I feel that it would be impolite not to laugh at his joke.

I ask Fidel how the U.S. trade embargo has affected the Cuban economy, hoping to get our interview back on track. Fidel offers me a sip of his whiskey and says, "I find your big belly amusing. It would please me to watch you dance." His soldiers begin firing their guns at my feet, which strikes me as very rude. But not wanting to displease Fidel, I dance for him. Fidel laughs again, slapping his knees and shouting, "Dance, fat boy, dance."

After several minutes of this entertainment, Fidel becomes bored. "Crawl on the floor, fat boy," Fidel stammers at me. "I am going to ride you like a horsey." I do as he says and Fidel sits on my back, making comical cowboy sounds and slapping my behind.

"Look at me ride the horsey," Fidel howls at his soldiers. "I am a cowboy! Yee-hay! I am John Wayne! I am riding on the prairie with my fat horsey!"

drive off into the city.

"Where are we going?" I ask.

"Shut your trap," one of the thugs yells. I do as I am told.

Upon arriving at Fidel's palace, I am whisked through double glass doors into a large, lavishly furnished reception room. The guards search me for weapons, checking every orifice thoroughly. I am not offended by their gropings. When you're as important as Fidel Castro, you can't afford to be too careful. After a complete physical examination, the guards are satisfied and inform me that Fidel will be with me shortly. I wait for three hours, trying my best not to lose my mind with anticipation.

And then the moment of truth arrives. A door opens and Fidel Castro walks inside. He is dressed in his olive-green military uniform and is surrounded by a large group of soldiers. He takes my hand and shakes it vigorously. He appears to be drunk, which is fine by me. Meeting Fidel in any condition is still a great honor.

We spend the first half hour getting acquainted, talking about Cuba, cigars and, much to my surprise, my magazine. He tells me that he is a big fan of *Cigar Asphyxianado*. He likes the articles, he says, but he would like to see "more photographs of big breasted women." I promise to bring up

Fidel let me peruse his private library, where he showed me his favorite book, The Kennedy Women. *"I read it to my grand-children when they visit," he told me affectionately. "Always they say, 'Señora Angie Dickinson! Read the chapter on Señora Angie Dickinson!'"*

Moved by his story, I break out my videocas-sette of The Prince of Tides, *which Castro had never seen. As the credits rolled two tear-filled hours later, Fidel turned to me and asked quietly, "If they love each other so, then why can't they be together?"*

I had no answer. And together we wept.

Fidel eventually warms up to me, and for the next few hours we talk and laugh like the closest of friends. Fidel reveals that he is not the monster the world believes he is, but an insecure man with very real emotions. We develop a relationship uncommon between journalists and communist leaders. "I like you," Fidel finally admits. "I have decided not to have you killed."

It is almost 3:00 A.M. when we finish, and Fidel thanks me for a wonderful evening. I am taken to the limo by his guards and they drive me back into town, where they blindfold me and dump me

Sharing our passion for cigars broke Fidel and I through to a higher level of communication, and we connected with an intensity that most males shun. Physical barriers broke down as we rubbed each other's feet and told stories about our fathers.

As we watched the sunrise in silence, Fidel and I came to see each other as kindred spirits on a journey of discovery: to find and smoke the ultimate stogie. In our final moments together, I vowed to return to this holiest of holy lands.

into a river. As I crawl back towards land and make my way to the airport, I consider how fortunate I am to have met the mythical Fidel Castro. How many Asphyxianados would have sold their own grandmothers into white slavery to have been in my shoes? Although it is only one night, it is an event that will be among my most cherished memories. Even if the trade embargo with Cuba is not ended in my lifetime, I can say that I smoked a real Cuban cigar and shook the hands of the man who helped create them. My life is complete.

¡Viva Cuba! ¡Viva Fidel Castro!

SIZE

DOES

MATTER

HOYO
DE MONTA
CIGARS

**It's not just a big cigar.
It's also a big penis.**

Sometimes

a cigar is just a cigar.

And sometimes it's a

big, flaming phallic

symbol. If you have

suppressed homo-

erotic tendencies or

a need to compensate

for your lack of sexual

endowment, Hoyo de

Monta Cigars are guar-

anteed to satisfy. They

come in a staggering

array of sizes, from

seven to twenty feet

long! You couldn't find

larger cigars if you tried.

Chicks With Sticks

A New Generation of Cigar-smoking Women Declare Their Respiratory Independence

LIZ MALONE

After years of appearing in small B films and countless failed TV pilots, Liz Malone is finally a star. She surprised audiences and critics alike with her scene-stealing portrayal of a trailer park psycho's girlfriend in the made-for-TV movie *Trailer Park Psycho*. And her new sitcom, *Extremely Lucy*, is the hottest show on television. So no one was prepared for the blow she would deliver to the Hollywood establishment at last summer's Emmy Awards. When she walked to the stage to accept her trophy for Best Actress, she was smoking a cigar.

"I don't know what the big deal was," says Malone. "I just wanted to celebrate, and enjoying a cigar seemed like the best way to do that. But everybody made such a big deal of it. You'd think that I'd walked up there naked."

She might as well *have* been naked, given the horrified reaction of the Emmy audience. Many of them openly booed. Some coughed loudly or screamed at her to extinguish her "filthy cigar." The award show ended early that evening because the producer feared that the "cigar incident" (as it would later be called) would

inspire a full-fledged riot.

"There were a lot of very angry people at that show," remembers Malone. "A producer at NBC walked up to me afterwards and told me that I'd never work in Hollywood again. I don't know why everyone was in such a tizzy about it. It was just a cigar. I guarantee you, if it was a *guy* up there with a cigar, he wouldn't have gotten the same reaction."

Although Malone may feel like an outsider, she is far from alone. Women all across the country (many of them famous celebrities) are

smoking cigars, and their numbers are growing every day. According to some cigar manufacturers, almost 30% of smokers are female, up 29.5% from last year. This trend is understandably disconcerting, especially for men. It seems like only yesterday that women were the cigar lover's biggest enemy, publicly denouncing cigars as a stinky and nasty habit. But suddenly women have joined the cigar revolution, puffing away on stogies with the enthusiasm of long-time Asphyxianados. Why have so many women changed their minds about cigars?

Liz continued smoking her stogie during the press conference after this year's Emmys. Defending her right to smoke, she called critical members of the media "pink-lunged sons-a-bitches."

STACI TOOL

"Cigars are about power," says grunge-rocker and riot grrrl *(sic)* Staci Tool. "When I have a big fat stogie in my mouth, I have all the power. Guys are always shocked when I smoke cigars onstage. It's like I'm saying to them, 'Hey, I'm one tough mama and if you don't get outta my way, I'm gonna put my foot up your ass.' It also helps me protect myself in the mosh pit. I don't get groped by guys as often if they think they might get a handful of hot tobacco flame."

Tool experienced first hand just how scandalous a cigar-smoking female can be when she was a guest on the *Late Nite With Lenoman* talk show. Host Lenny Lenoman was clearly frightened by the huge cigar Tool smoked during the interview. Since her appearance, Tool has been banned from appearing on the show. She is not surprised by the decision, insisting that she was black-listed because "men are naturally fearful of a confident, smoking woman." She does concede, however, that the ban might also be because she accidentally set fire to the set with her cigar.

"I like to smoke big cigars and they can be difficult to hold on to," she says. "I guess I still have a lot to learn about smoking."

Staci Tool loves to smoke while performing, and has even gone as far as singing entire songs without taking her cigar out of her mouth. As one adoring fan put it, "With lyrics as powerful as Staci's, you don't NEED to hear the consonants."

NANCY BELLMARK

One woman who doesn't need any cigar instruction is Nancy Bellmark, the president and CEO of A&M Advertising. Bellmark has been a cigar smoker for twenty years. It is a habit that has helped her become the richest and most successful female businesswoman in the world.

"Men are scared of cigars," Bellmark says. "When I walk into a meeting with a lit cigar, I can see the fear in their eyes. They're petrified. Some of them literally start screaming and run out of the room. I've even made the occasional man cry. I figured out long ago that whenever I smoked cigars, men were more likely to give me respect."

Nancy's unique style of management has paid off for A&M Advertising. The once faltering firm now boasts an expanded client base, a 240% increase in productivity, and perfect employee attendance.

MADAME DUNHILL

Another successful business-woman who knows what Bellmark is talking about is Madame Dunhill, a professional dominatrix who has turned her love of cigars into a lucrative career. As a woman paid to intimidate and punish men, she finds that cigars make her job easier.

"Whether they're smokers themselves or not, men feel intimidated by women who smoke cigars," says Dunhill. "There's just something frightening about an attractive woman with a big, wet, nasty-smelling stogie hanging from her mouth. You demonstrate right from the start that you're the one in charge. And men know what a cigar *really* means. It says to them, 'I have a bigger penis than you.' They get the message loud and clear."

With a clientele ranging from Hollywood brat packers to prominent televangelists, Madame Dunhill makes anonymity a strict priority. She even refused to allow us to photograph this subject from any angle which might show his face. Quote Dunhill, "I'm a professional, and I would never reveal a client's name. But I can tell you his rhymes with 'Toot Gingrich.'"

Shirley Jones proudly shows off the scar from her recent surgery. "No one should feel sorry for me because I lost a lung," says Jones. "It's those pansies who need two lungs that deserve all the sympathy."

Not all women smoke cigars just to intimidate men. Some enjoy the reactions they get from their fellow women. Tennis pro Shirley Jones is a veteran cigar smoker and currently the game's No. 1 player.

"When I walk onto the court with my cigar, my opponent usually thinks I'm crazy," says Jones. "I guess I can understand why. I am the only smoker on the woman's tour. But I'm also the biggest winner. Usually my opponents take one look at me

with a cigar, coughing and hacking up big globs of phlegm, and they totally lose their competitive edge. I guess they assume that anybody with so little lung capacity must have some kind of secret weapon."

Despite Jones' winning streak, the Women's Tennis Association still insists that smoking is detrimental. They cite evidence that smoking is unhealthy and consistently refuse to endorse the use of cigars by other female athletes.

But Jones has proven them all wrong, winning almost every major tennis tournament this year, including the French Open and Wimbledon. It's a remarkable achievement for Jones, especially considering that she underwent surgery just last summer to have her right lung removed.

"I couldn't have won those games alone," says Jones, a little wistfully. "I owe everything to my cigars. They were with me every step of the way."

LANA McDONALD

Cigar-smoking cover girl Lana McDonald also loves a good stogie. McDonald is the most popular swimsuit model in the world, gracing the covers of over three thousand magazines. She also recently opened her own bikini-themed restaurant in New York. But it isn't her stunning good looks or gorgeous body that has made

McDonald an international superstar. According to McDonald, the key to her sex appeal is cigar-smoking.

"At first I just smoked cigars for fun," says McDonald. "I'd have a cigar or two during my breaks or when I was on vacation. But after a while I was smoking *all* the time. And I was belligerent about it. I'd

smoke cigars at my photo shoots and refuse to stop when the cameras were rolling. I told them that they'd have to take a picture of me with a cigar or not at all. I wasn't putting out my cigar for anybody!"

As it turned out, McDonald's love for cigars paid off. Her now infamous "cigar babe"

Lana McDonald claims that smoking cigars has helped her maintain her supermodel figure. "I can get a great workout from the really big cigars," says McDonald. "I tend to smoke cigars that weigh up to 60 and 70 pounds. Those things can break your neck if you're not careful."

photo spread in *Sport Bikini Spectacular* magazine flew off the newsstands in record numbers, and fashion insiders predicted that women and cigars would soon be the hottest trend of the decade. Before long, cigars and swimsuits became inseparable in the fashion industry. Hundreds of models copied McDonald's cigar-smoking look, and cigars are now a required accessory in the major fashion shows of London, Paris, and New York.

Even the most dubious critics of the cigar fashion craze have changed their tunes. "It's definitely hip," says Alex DuBois, the world renowned fashion designer. "At first I was a little doubtful. Didn't seem hip to me at all. But then I saw a few shows in London that featured cigars and I thought, 'This could become hip.' Then I realized I was the only designer who *wasn't* using cigars and I was convinced. I said to myself, 'This is hip.' And I was *right*."

Although women who smoke cigars may only feel totally welcome in the fashion industry, the rest of the world is slowly, but surely, catching on. Hollywood is releasing five new movies over the next year with cigar-smoking female leads. Other stogie-friendly rockers like Staci Tool are finally being given record deals. And even on TV, where cigar-smoking women have typically been outcast, there are signs that the bias against cigars is finally a thing of the past.

"There's been talk among the network executives of turning my character into a smoker," says Liz Malone of her role on *Extremely Lucy*. "I think that'd be a huge step not just for cigar smokers but for women in general. A lot of women smoke cigars, and it's time that television reflected that. I realize that it'd be a big step for my character to come out of the closet and admit her fondness for nicotine, but it's a chance I'm willing to take. I think audiences would be open to a female smoker. I mean c'mon, it's the 90s."

But what if the mania over women and cigars ends tomorrow? Will Malone stop smoking and start acting like the respectable, demure female that's expected of her? Malone just laughs, coughs wildly and spits an alarming amount of mucus from her mouth.

"Not a chance," she says with a smile. "Cigars will never go out of style."

Designer Alex DuBois (above) is now hard at work on his summer line, which will feature dresses made entirely of tobacco leaves.
Wearing a DuBois original at the Emmy's, Liz Malone (below) was evasive as to whether or not her character on Extremely Lucy *was a smoker or not. Says Malone, "What Lucy smokes is no more important than, say, what type of woman she likes to date."*

So You Want to Buy a Private ISLAND

There's something undeniably romantic about owning an island. Who wouldn't want to live in a tropical paradise with white sandy beaches, idyllic azure coves, and mile after mile of beautiful places to smoke? It is the perfect getaway for an Asphyxianado who has grown weary of life among the masses.

But just how does one go about buying a private island? According to Franz Vlada, one of the most successful island brokers in the business, it isn't as difficult as you'd think. All you need is some ready cash, a love of solitude, and a willingness to subsist entirely on coconuts and shrubbery.

"You'd be surprised at how many people come to me looking to buy an island," Vlada says. "It's fairly typical these days, and with good reason. Islands are a much better investment than a house, because you're guaranteed privacy. You won't have salesmen, the government or even relatives making unexpected visits, unless they have a boat or something. And if you're a cigar smoker — as most of my customers are — an island has a lot of obvious benefits. You can enjoy as many cigars as you want and you'll never have an irritable non-smoker ruining your fun. It's your island, so everywhere is a smoking section."

Vlada says that there are only two simple steps to buying an island. First, get a large sum of money, somewhere around 500 million dollars. Next, find an island that fits your personality. Do you want a remote hideaway that offers you relaxation and peace? Or do you want an island with a little more pizzazz, someplace where there is the constant danger of destruction by tornadoes, floods, or violent natives? Legal consultant Neil Barber opted for the latter, and he has never regretted it. His island in New Zealand is inhabited by a vicious tribe of head hunters who have kidnapped and mur-

dered his last four wives. "It makes life really exciting for me," says Barber. "You never know when some of them damn savages are going to bust down your doors and try to scalp you. It keeps you on your toes and ensures that you'll never get bored. It's worked out really well for me. I never have to get divorced because whenever I want to leave my wife, it's a good bet that sooner or later she'll be snatched up by a head-hunter. I'd say that this island has kept me young."

But even if you find an island that's right for you, that doesn't necessarily mean that it'll be for sale. Vlada says that only

400 islands are currently available, and not all of them are in the best condition. "A lot of these islands are owned by countries in the midst of revolutions or political upheavals," says Vlada. "I've got some great properties in Panama, but all the bloody fighting down there can make it difficult for new owners to get settled. If you're willing to put up with the occasional bombing and rebels using your house to store weapons, you can get a great deal."

Another factor that a potential island inhabitant should consider is how he or she will adapt to life in a remote location. Vlada warns that living on an island is a major and often traumatic adjustment. Some of the most basic necessities of life — like food, clothing, and shelter — are difficult to come by when you're out in the middle

of nowhere. "You won't be able to rent a movie or buy a newspaper," says Vlada. "You could always open your own convenience store, but that can be time-consuming and, let's face it, not very profitable. You'll be your only customer, and you probably won't buy enough to keep yourself in business."

There's also the separation factor, that all-too-common sense of seclusion, which causes many island dwellers serious mental distress. Advertising director Lucy Streisberg owned an island in the Caribbean with her husband, but after only six months of living in her tropical paradise, her husband started to lose his mind because of "isolation jitters."

"He really started to flip out on me," says Streisberg. "He'd disappear for days in the jungle and return covered in boar

blood and mumbling that he had fought for my honor. He stopped wearing clothes, started covering his body in fig leaves and soot, and demanded that I call him 'Zortar, Lord of Fertility and the Harvest.' I guess he just wasn't comfortable being on an island without the comforts of civilization. But we've already made the down payment so there's no going back. If I had known that my husband would turn into a *Lord of the Flies* character, we never would have bought the island in the first place. But at this point, it's too late to get out of it. For better or for worse, we're stuck with it."

Vlada suggests that before you make the big purchase, you should first determine whether your lifestyle is suited for island ownership. Vlada gives the same advice to all of his prospective buyers: rent first, buy later.

"You can rent islands for a fraction of the cost of buying them," says Vlada. "There are some superb islands in the Fijis and Bahamas that rent for only $2 million a month. I know of a few islands in the Maldives that have bungalows on glistening white beaches, and they only cost around $800,000 a week. If money is a problem, there are some great islands which only cost $200,000 a week. They have thick tropical vegetation and greenish-blue lagoons. The only drawback is that they just happen to be in the middle of popular drug-smuggling routes. But the odds are against you getting gunned downed as long as you stay indoors and don't make any loud noises."

Vlada urges shoppers to think long and hard about the costs of buying an island before writing a check. "It's easy to forget about the expenses when weighed against the common fantasy of island life," says Vlada. "Everybody wants to live among sun-drenched palms and lagoons, where voluptuous, barely-clad island girls serve you drinks and fan you all day. You can get that, but it's going to cost you extra. Too many people think that buying an island is a just one-time expense. But after you shell out the money for the island, that's just the beginning. You have to pay for a telephone permit, a caretaker, and artillery to protect yourself from hostile natives and animals. You'll probably also have to build a wharf and an airstrip. And then there are all the government bribes. After adding up all the costs, it's a lot like running your own country."

But Vlada insists that buying an island is still the best purchase that an Asphyxianado can make. "If it's important enough to you, you can make it happen," says Vlada. "You may have to cut a few corners; mortgage your house, steal from your family, maybe do a little money laundering or embezzlement. Don't pay your taxes for a few years and see how much you can save. The IRS might not like it, but once you're living on your own island, there's no way they can touch you."

Vlada has owned his own island for twenty years, and he claims that it has provided him with some of the most precious memories of his life. "There's no better pleasure than sitting naked on a beach, overlooking crystal-clear blue water, watching some unwelcome visitors get slowly devoured by sharks, and smoking a box of my favorite cigars. It makes all the hassles worth it."

The best way to say "You're fired!"

It's hard to be the boss. You have
to make the tough decisions.
And sometimes, regrettably,
you have to fire your employees.
But with a Gesta Rey Cigar, being
an unfeeling bastard is easy. Gesta
Rey Cigars make you feel powerful and in charge, so you don't
mind telling that lazy S.O.B. with
the family to support that he's
gotta clean out his desk and
never come back. You may be
a good person at heart, but with
a Gesta Rey Cigar, nobody will
ever know.

GESTA REY CIGARS
We'll help you do the dirty work.

"It's my PARTY and I'll SMOKE if I want to!"

Behind the Scenes at the Big Stogie VII

Each year *Cigar Asphyxianado* hosts a gala party to celebrate cigars and the people who love them. We call it "The Big Stogie" and it is one of the most prestigious cigar events in the world. Those lucky souls who made it to this year's Big Stogie experienced a historic occasion that will undoubtedly be the most treasured memory of their short lives. For a mere $2000 admission charge, guests were able to mingle with other cigar lovers, enjoy fine food

Noted cigar expert Alfonso Nitti dances intimately with his wife Psimone Carlisle, the former Duchess of Gloucester. The pair were undoubtedly celebrating being recently named "The Most Arrogant Couple Alive" by Peoplewatcher Magazine.

Pamela Sue Henderson demonstrates the motor skills which landed her on the international syndicated hit Lifeguard Babes. *Moments after this photograph was taken, a small fire caught in Pamela's boa. Thinking quickly, Pamela threw it on the floor and sent her personal trainer to get her spare boa from the Jag.*

and drink, attend a variety of fascinating seminars, and smoke enough cigars to make even the most experienced smoker pass out from lack of oxygen.

The party was held at a posh hotel in Chicago (which, for reasons unknown to us, wishes to remain nameless). Over three thousand cigar smokers showed up for the festivities, including politicians, movie stars, sports icons, and distributors of some of the biggest and most expensive cigar brands on the market.

Cigar Asphyxianado's publisher Marty Scanken began the evening with an inspiring speech, reminding the crowd how remarkable it was that cigars have become so popular.

"When I first got the idea to start this magazine, people told me it wouldn't last," he said. "They laughed at me and called me names. Some of them even tackled me to the ground and tried to make me cry like a girl. My own parents threatened to kick me out of the house. I didn't listen to any of them, and now I'm the one laughing."

Francis Talese, the Pulitzer Prize-winning author and passionate lover of cigars, also gave a speech to the crowd, waxing poetic about the romance of smoking too many cigars. "This is truly a magical evening for Cigar Asphyxianados," he said between violent bouts of coughing. "I've smoked over fifty cigars already and I'm not going to quit until I've smoked a hundred more!" The crowd applauded wildly as Mr. Talese collapsed on the stage and was rushed to the hospital.

Following the introductions, guests were treated to an elegant four-course dinner consisting of lobster, steak, and French wine. It was reportedly a very delicious meal, although none of the devout smokers had enough oral sensation to taste the cuisine. After dinner, guests retreated to the mezzanine to smoke more cigars and attend seminars on a number of cigar-related topics such as "Cigar-making: Construction and Quality Control," "Wrapper Selection," "Cigar Appreciation," and "Cigars and Sex: Sometimes a Cigar Is Just a Big, Flaming Penis."

In keeping with Big Stogie tradition, Marty Scanken drank far too

Designer Alex DuBois (center) was on hand to give the guests plenty of unwanted fashion advice. As this photo was taken, DuBois was heard to remark "Darling, the grunge look is so five minutes ago" before being slugged.

Cigar guru Del Farr made a rare appearance to give the keynote address at Big Stogie VII. Unfortunately, Del was high as a satellite from some "bad Guatemalan leaf," and most of his speech devolved into telling old stories about "nailing chicks with Groucho."

Alfonso Nitti scans the room for his wife while Del Farr speculates upon the behavior of cigar smoke in extradimensional realities.

Howie Fleischmann, self-proclaimed "Pimp of Hollywood," negotiates a commission with a lovely lady from his escort service. "Being the boss," says Howie to would-be pimps, "means sometimes making difficult human resource decisions."

CA Editor-in-chief and Master of Ceremonies Marty Scanken tossed his cookies after an hour of drinking and smoking, much to the chagrin of Dinner for 6 teen heartthrob Joey Sperando and his legal guardian Aunt Stella Sperando.

Author Francis Talese only moments before his tragic collapse. According to friends, he seemed "fine" and had been "backing away just like normal" the entire evening.

In a scandalous turn, CA's Marty Scanken put the make on Psimone Carlisle. She stuanchly resisted his repeated request to "lick her wrapper."

Brat Packer Arty McAndrew gets his fortune told by Tejano Super-psychic Monica Bravo. McAndrew listened attentively to Bravo's prediction that "a new path and a healthy percentage" await him in the field of infomercials.

Alfonso Nitti confronts Marty Scanken on his unwanted advances towards his wife, Psimone. Marty vehemently denied any ill intent, claiming that he was misunderstood and had only asked her for a "nice piece of ash."

Disgusted by the lack of paparazzi, Henderson and DuBois left the party early. "Everybody's too busy smoking cigars to gawk at me," said Henderson. "I feel so...unviolated."

Monica Bravo demonstrates an ancient Mayan technique of exorcizing demons using energy projected from the open palm. Willing subjects like Howie Fleischmann pay up to $400 for a single such healing session with Bravo.

Having jointly and separately offended every individual attendee at Big Stogie VII, Scanken was finally asked to leave the festivities. He is shown above being escorted out by Monica Bravo and caucasian rap sensation L.L. White Bread.

much whiskey and made embarrassing comments that will haunt him for some time. "I'm rich! I'm rich!" He screamed at guests, despite efforts by his associates to calm him down. "You fools! I can't believe you buy into this crap! It's a goddamn magazine about cigars, for Christ's sake! You're all idiots! I'm rich! Look at all my money!"

The only sour note of the evening occurred after midnight, when the "non-smoking" guests at the hotel began complaining about the massive cloud of carcinogenic smoke and the management asked the Big Stogie's guests to leave. The party was moved to the parking lot where it continued into the wee hours of the morning without a hitch, despite the strong winds and hail. The guests refused to let the adverse conditions ruin their night of smoking and enjoying fine cigars.

"I've been looking forward to this party all year," said one guest. "I wouldn't miss a second of it, regardless of where it's held. I had to quit my job and divorce my wife to get here, so there's no way I'm gonna let a little freezing rain stop me."

THE CIGAR EXPERT

Alfonso Nitti
The Godfather of Cigar Etiquette

Dear Cigar Expert,

I've often heard that the only way to experience a premium cigar is by using all of your senses; specifically sight, smell, and taste. I have attempted to do this but have had little success. Most cigars tend to deaden my senses rather than stimulate them. Any suggestions?
— Senseless in Seattle

Dear Senseless,

This nonsense about "using the senses" has plagued the cigar world for far too long. A truly fine cigar cannot possibly be experienced with smell or taste. If the cigars you've been smoking were any good, the smoke would have been so thick and noxious that it clogged your nostrils like cement. The best cigars trigger symptoms similar to that of a common cold. The eyes water, the nose runs, the chest feels congested and a fever may develop. Some smokers like to enjoy their cigars with a NyQuil cocktail, but purists insist that this is cheating. Submitting yourself to such sensory pummeling may seem pointless, but the astute Asphyxianado understands that a premium cigar is an enigma. We can never hope to understand its mysterious purpose. In other words, shut your trap and take it like a man.

Dear Cigar Expert,

I recently visited a tobacconist and was shocked to discover that there are virtually hundreds of different cigar brands to choose from. I tried to make an intelligent selection, but I had no idea how to determine which cigars had the best quality. Do you have any tips for novice smokers who can't tell the difference between a premium cigar and a sucky one?
— Dumb in Chicago

Dear Dumb,

The only way to determine the quality of a cigar is by fondling it. Begin by inspecting the cigar from top to bottom, running your hands along its silky wrapper and checking it thoroughly for blemishes. Note the texture of its wrapper, squeeze the center to test its firmness, and throw it to the ground to see if it bounces.

Caress it like you would a lover, albeit a lover that you intend to set on fire and inhale its remains. Hold the cigar under a strong light and examine its color, which should be either green (claro) or black (oscuro). If it has a different color, like red or pink, then it is probably not a real cigar at all but actually a "candy cigar." If this is the case, it should be eaten and not smoked. A properly stored cigar will be firm yet resilient. When gently squeezed, the cigar should make almost no sound. Any significant crackling means that the cigar is too dry. If it squeaks like a child's play-toy, than the cigar is probably constructed from rubber. Continue examining the cigar until you are satisfied that it is in pristine condition, or until you are convinced that everybody in the room is impressed with your skills, whichever comes first.

Dear Cigar Expert,

Are cigars made in the Dominican Republic better than cigars made in America? I've heard a lot of discussion on this topic but I have yet to be convinced either way. What is your opinion?

— Too Much Free Time in Ohio

Dear Free Time,

One of the most persistent myths about cigars is that a stogie's quality is directly related to the country that produced it. This is absolute horseshit and you're a fool to believe it. The only indicator of a cigar's quality is how cool the brand name sounds. A cigar with a fancy foreign name is naturally going to be better tasting than a cigar with a short, dull name. A cigar like "Habana Gold" is probably not very good, simply because the name is so ordinary. But a cigar with a name like "Arturo Fuente Flor Fina 8-5-8 Robusto Maduro No. 500" is not just difficult to pronounce, it's also a sign that this cigar is really expensive and may even be impossible to purchase without breaking a few international laws. Use this rule of thumb when picking your cigars: If you can't say the brand name

without garbling the words, then it is likely that this cigar is not worthy of your time and money.

Dear Cigar Expert

I have always enjoyed cigars, but I am disturbed by the alarming amount of phlegm that usually results from a satisfying smoke. Is this normal?

— Too Much Mucus in Chicago

Dear Mucus,

Cigars and phlegm go hand in hand, and Asphyxianados realize that the only way to judge a premium cigar is by the quality and quantity of the phlegm it produces. The phlegm from a great cigar is a work of art, transparent and gooey and tasting like warm licorice. Never be shy about sharing your phlegm with others. It is quite common to see a group of smokers gathered together, puffing happily on their stogies and pausing every so often to spit large volumes of mucus from their mouths. If they're doing more spitting than smoking, you know they have some really good cigars. If a cigar is a gift from a friend, hacking a big glob of phlegm onto his shoes is considered the highest form of flattery. The only downside to a mouthful of phlegm is that sometimes it can wet down a cigar too much, causing it to extinguish prematurely. If this

happens, do not re-light your cigar. It is considered bad form to do so, especially in phlegm-related cases. It's always better to continue puffing on your cigar, and if a fellow smoker questions your behavior, just look at him and say "phlegm." If he's any kind of Asphyxianado, he'll know exactly what you're talking about, and he'll respect you more for it.

Dear Cigar Expert,

Are big cigars better than small cigars?

— Insecure in Minneapolis

Dear Insecure,

I always recommend bigger cigars, mostly because they offer a richer and fuller flavor. But in addition to allowing more complex blending, the size of a cigar governs how long it will last. Big cigars naturally last longer, sometimes as long as 120 minutes. And the longer a cigar lasts, the better the chances that someone will see you with it and admire how hip you are for being an Asphyxianado. Many smokers are intimidated by large ring-gauge cigars, but these people are pansies and should be laughed at in public as often as possible. If you are afraid of larger-sized cigars, my suspicion is that you have a very small penis. As anybody can tell you, the bigger the cigar...

"One hundred years ago, our great-great grandfather had a **dream**. He set out to make a cigar worthy to share the name and heritage of the Martinez **family**. After a lifetime spent in pursuit of excellence, he created **El Martinezo**, a cigar with the finest blend of rich tobacco anywhere in the world. He passed on his secrets to his **children**, and they to their children. And now we have inherited the proud Martinez tradition of cigar **perfection**."

"But we're **greedy**, so we sold our share of the family business to the **highest bidder**. You won't find us sweating our **asses** off in the middle of some godforsaken tobacco field. We're moving to **Hawaii**!"

El *Martinezo*
C I G A R S
Smoke the very best...or don't. We get paid either way.

COUGHING HER WAY TO OLYMPIC GLORY

by Bela Karolini

It is the dream of every gymnastic coach to someday win an Olympic championship. During my forty-year career I struggled valiantly to lead the U.S. women's gymnastic team to a gold medal but had little success. Then in 1996, my dreams became a reality, thanks to the "never-say-die" attitude of a fearless young girl and a box of El Rey Del Mundo premium cigars.

It was a hot and smarmy August night at the Georgia Dome and the Olympic gymnastic finals were turning into a blood bath. The Russians were beating our asses in every event. The air was thick with tension and — not surprisingly — thick clouds of cigar smoke. I have been a cigar smoker for as long as I've coached Olympic gymnastics. I find that smoking helps me relax when the stress becomes unbearable. On this dreadful evening, my cigars were the only things keeping me from losing my cool and smacking around those weak girls.

The last hope for an American victory was a solid performance on the vault. The first four girls flipped safely, but the judges were not impressed. Then 14-year-old Carrie Strog took to the runway and, in a tragic development, fell on her fat ass and sprawled like a dead fish on the mat, scoring a wretched 9.1.

Bela Karolini inspires young Carrie Strog only moments after her disastrous ankle injury at the 1996 Olympics. The phrase "Win for Bela! Smoke for Bela!" is a rallying cry that has brought out the best in young girls on both sides of the former Iron Curtain.

The rabid, gold-hungry crowd quieted down. Nobody in the arena noticed that Strog had rolled on her ankle and snapped it like a toothpick. I urged her to shake it off as she hobbled back onto her feet. I felt the gold medal was slipping away and I refused to let it happen without a fight. Strog cried out that she was in pain and couldn't make the second vault. I knew that I would have to take decisive action or we would lose the Olympics in a terrible and humiliating defeat.

I handed Strog one of my El Rey Del Mundo cigars and instructed her to smoke it. At first she resisted, telling me that she had been raised never to smoke nicotine of any kind. But after some persuasive intimidation and name-calling, she agreed to smoke the cigar. "Suck it in," I screamed as she eagerly puffed on the big stogie. "Don't let any of the smoke out. Suck it all into your lungs." After finishing the cigar, she experienced such a head buzz that she didn't even remember her name, much less the pain in her leg. She went back out onto the runway and completed a spectacular vault that will be remembered as one of the most heroic moments in Olympic history.

After her jump, medics wanted to rush her to the hospital. But I wouldn't hear of it. "Not even the surgeon general can stop me from taking you up," I told her as I swept her up in my arms and

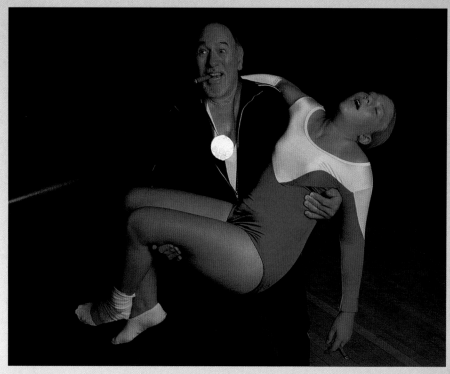

Karolini proudly wears the Olympic Gold after Carrie Strog's dramatic victory. Sadly, Carrie enjoyed none of the accolades medalists usually receive due to a three-week coma.

carried her pale and lifeless body to the medal podium. "It hurts," she told me as tears filled her eyes. "Carrie," I said. "You're an Olympic champion now. Enjoy it. Have another cigar!"

I know that some critics have condemned my coaching methods, claiming that I abused young Strog by bullying her to perform with a broken leg. But it was not I who made Strog ignore the throbbing pain and vault her way to victory. It was the cigar. If it wasn't for the "tough love" of nicotine, Strog would just be another permanently crippled child who had tried and failed to win at the Olympics. But now, as

she sits in her wheelchair and hacks up black chunks of what is left of her lungs, she will be able to look at her gold medal and remember that she had the courage to defy the odds.

I have heard that Strog is hoping to compete for UCLA in the coming year. And if my unreturned phone calls are any indication, she may very well be looking for a new coach. I fear that she has gone soft, giving in to the pressure of coddling parents who are fearful of the stern leadership that only I can provide. But whatever her decision may be, her place in Olympic history is secure. She will always be remembered as a brave girl who took one gallant leap — and one gallant cigar — for glory!

CREDITS

Written by Eric Spitznagel

Art Direction by Michael Ross

Photographs by Marty Perez

Illustrations by George Eckart

Captions by Michael Ross & Eric Spitznagel

MODELS

Monica Bravo, Mike Brumm, William Canavan, Shulie Cowen, Matthew Craig, Matt Cullison, Dina Facklis, Matthew Favazza, Brian Fazio, Jason Flowers, Michael Gellman, Kenn Goodman, Michael Grollman, Jennifer Holland, Claudine Hennessey, T.J. Jagodowski, John Kelly, Henry Klotkowski, Laura Krafft, Kelly Kreglow, Katie Landfear, Danielle Leyshon, Bob Lukens, Carmen Marrero, Jacobina Martin, Jim McMahon, Jonathan Meehan, Joel Mehr, Joe Nunez, Jenny Overmeyer, Monica Payne, Rosemarie Perez-Pelaez, Stuart Ranson, Rachel Romanski, Jack Ross, John Ross, Katie Ross, Kevin Ross, Michael Ross, John Rusch, Patricia Rusch, Horacio Sanz, Eric Spitznagel, Jocelyn Swafford, Carrie Vann.

SPECIAL THANKS

The Second City, Rob McMahon, Anna Maria Piluso, Diane Luger, Dan Mandel, Up-Down Tobacco Shop, Jane Jordan Browne and everyone at Multimedia Product Development, Martin C. Wojcik and Troy Clampit at Litho Prep, Rich Ross, Yakzies Bar, *Runner's World* magazine, Andrew Alexander, Kelly Leonard, the E.T.C. cast, Lounge Ax, ImprovOlympic, Dick Cohen, Paul Ristau, Cathy Galati, Kelly & Barbara Kreglow, Merle Grollman, Brendan Baber, Sam Mednick, Kathy Jones, Jim McMahon, Brendan Gardiner, and the Chicago Park District.